DISCARD

Bodies and Brains

WORLD
BOOK

www.worldbook.com

World Book, Inc.
180 North LaSalle Street
Suite 900
Chicago, Illinois 60601
USA

For information about other World Book publications, visit our website at www.worldbook.com or call 1-800-WORLDBK (967-5325).

For information about sales to schools and libraries, call 1-800-975-3250 (United States), or 1-800-837-5365 (Canada).

Library of Congress Cataloging-in-Publication Data for this volume has been applied for.

This edition: ISBN: 978-0-7166-4060-8 (hc.)
ISBN: 978-0-7166-4056-1 (set, hc.)

Also available as: ISBN: 978-0-7166-4066-0 (e-book)

Printed in China by Shenzhen Wing King Tong Paper Products Co., Ltd., Shenzhen, Guangdong
1st printing July 2018

Produced for World Book by White-Thomson Publishing Ltd

www.wtpub.co.uk

Author: Paul Harrison
Editor: Izzi Howell
Design/Art director: Claire Gaukrodger
Illustrator: Rob Davis/The Art Agency

Cover artwork: © Doug Holgate

Staff

A glossary of terms appears on p. 94.

Contents

Zac Newton and friends

Zac is a junior genius and inventor of the Backspace app. The app allows Zac and his friends to take virtual trips through time and space, just by snapping a selfie.

Lucía has a sharp mind and an even sharper wit. She pretends to be too cool for school, but inside she burns to learn about science.

Quick-thinking Marcus is always ready with a joke. Although he loves to clown around, he knows more than he lets on.

Ning likes to run, jump, and play ball. She may be the youngest of the group, but nobody's going to push her around.

Zac's dog, Orbit, loves to join Zac and his friends on their adventures. He's not afraid of anything—except loud noises.

Chapter 1
Stardust

One afternoon, Zac, Lucía, and Ning were hanging out in Zac's basement. Zac and Lucía were sorting through some old comic books. Zac's dog, Orbit, lounged nearby. Ning was showing off her gymnastics moves. With an easy twist, she spun head over heels, landing gracefully back on her feet.

"See! It's easy!" she said. "Anyone can do it."

"I doubt that!" said Lucía, looking up. "I can't even do a cartwheel." She laughed.

"What? You've got to be kidding me! You can't do a cartwheel?" said Ning. "Come on, I can teach you. It's easy."

"No, that's okay, thanks," Lucía replied. "I've gotten this far in life without being able to do a cartwheel. I bet I'll be fine."

"I think you're just scared." Ning smiled.

Suddenly, the door to the basement swung open, and Marcus entered. Usually, Marcus sprang eagerly down the steps. But today, he shuffled heavily to the bottom and flopped into a chair. Zac, Lucía, and Ning glanced at one another, puzzled.

"Hey, Marcus, how's it going?" said Zac.

"Worst day eber," sniffled Marcus. "I have a cold, and it's giving me a thtuffy doze."

"What did he say?" asked Ning.

"I thaid I have a…a…a…ACHOO!" Marcus let out an explosive sneeze. He wiped his face on his sleeve. "Ah, that's better," he said.

"Urrrggghhhh! That's so disgusting," said Lucía.

"What? It's not my fault I have a cold," Marcus complained.

"But you just sprayed germs everywhere! Then, to make it worse, you wiped your nose on your sleeve!" Lucía protested.

"ACHOO!" Marcus sneezed again.

"Oh, I've had enough of this!" huffed Lucía. "Ning, let's go outside. You can teach me how to do a cartwheel. I'd rather risk breaking my neck than catch his germs!"

"Seriously?" said Ning.

"Well, I'm guaranteed to catch a cold staying here. I'll take my chances with you in the fresh air. Let's go."

The girls headed off upstairs. Orbit hurried after them with an excited "Woof!"

"Looks like Orbit has had enough of your sneezing, too," Zac joked.

"Sneezing is the least of my worries," said Marcus. "I have a science project to finish. Unless I can come up with a better idea, I'll have to make another baking soda volcano."

"A baking soda volcano? You made one of those last year! We can think of something new and exciting!" Zac exclaimed.

"Like… a…a…a…ACHOO…. Like what?"

"Ha! That gives me an idea. We can make the project about you," said Zac.

"Me? What do you mean? Like how awesome I am?" joked Marcus.

"Well, kind of. You are awesome, really," said Zac.

"Well, I always figured that was true," said Marcus. But I'm glad you finally noticed."

"No, I don't mean it like that," said Zac. "What I mean is that we're all awesome. Your body—the human body—is an amazing and complex thing. You could do a project on that."

"Can I just stop you there? You said the word *complex*, Zac. That doesn't sound easy. Baking soda volcanoes—now those are very, very easy. And, to be clear, I like easy."

"And do you like bad grades, too?" Zac replied. "You can't do another volcano. Just because the body is complex, it doesn't mean your project has to be."

"Really?" Marcus replied doubtfully.

"Really. Let me demonstrate." Zac grabbed his cell phone and held it up, preparing to take a selfie with Marcus. "You remember the Backspace app I invented? It can take us on a virtual visit to any point in history, just by snapping a selfie."

"Yep, I remember," replied Marcus.

"Well, it can also show us any scene, anywhere, at any time, right up to the present day. And that's where we're going now."

"But we're already in the present day," Marcus protested.

"Just you wait," replied Zac, "and prepare to be amazed!"

Zac tapped the Backspace button on the screen.

FLASH!

ZUMMMMMMMmmmmmmm...

A bright light flashed before their eyes, and the scene around them changed. They were no longer surrounded by the familiar sights of Zac's basement. Instead, the two friends appeared to be floating in outer space. They were inside a cloud of dust that stretched as far as the eye could see. In the distance, blurry dots of light glowed through the haze.

"Where are we?" Marcus asked.

"This is the Orion Nebula," explained Zac. "You can see it from my yard. It doesn't look like this from that far away, though. From there, it looks more like a small, cloudy star in the constellation Orion."

"The Orion what-ula?" asked Marcus.

"Nebula," said Zac, pronouncing it slowly. "*NEHB yuh luh.* It's a huge cloud of dust and gas. There are lots of them. And some of them, including this one, are where new stars are born."

Zac pointed to one of the hazy lights. The friends gazed upon the newborn star in awe.

"This is amazing and everything," said Marcus, "but what does it have to do with my science project? I thought you said I should do something about the human body, not outer space."

"I did," said Zac. "I'm showing you this to get you excited about your project. You see, we're made from this stuff, too."

"What?" exclaimed Marcus. "We're made of… stardust?"

"In a way, yes. Like all matter, people are made up of chemical elements—things like carbon and oxygen and nitrogen. All of these elements come from space. Nearly all are formed in the hearts of stars."

"So, I really am a star, after all," smiled Marcus.

"Typical," sighed Zac. He closed the app, and the friends were once again in Zac's basement.

"Seriously though," said Marcus, "that was mind-blowing! It's too bad Lucía and Ning weren't here to see it. I suppose it serves them right for being scared of a little sneeze."

"Well, they did have a point," said Zac. "You see, the reason the body sneezes is to…"

Before Zac could finish, the door to the basement burst open, and Lucía dashed in. She looked worried.

"Quick!" she shouted. "Ning's had an accident. She looks hurt!"

Chapter 2
Ning's Big Break

Zac, Lucía, and Marcus sat in the waiting room at the hospital, hoping to hear if Ning was okay. It was so quiet that they hardly dared to make a sound.

"So, tell me again…" Zac began. The adults in the waiting room looked over suddenly. He lowered his voice. "What happened exactly, Lucía?"

Lucía sighed. "We went out to the front yard to get away from Marcus and his germs." She gave Marcus a dirty look. He raised his hands in protest. "Anyway, Ning was showing me how to do cartwheels. She did some, and then I tried to do a couple. Then she did a couple more, because I wasn't getting it. On the last one, she tripped over Orbit and landed on her arm."

"At least Orbit is okay," said Marcus.

"He thought it was part of a game," said Lucía. "Until Ning started crying, that is. Then he looked really sad, like he felt guilty."

"Poor Orbit," said Zac.

"Never mind poor Orbit. What about poor Ning?!" came a voice. The friends spun around in their seats to see Ning coming into the room with her mother.

"Hey, Ning!" said Zac. "How are you?"

"Oh, I'm fine, I guess. My arm doesn't hurt as much as it did. I have to go for an X-ray examination in a minute, so I thought I'd find you to tell you what's happening."

"Honey, I'm just going to grab a coffee from that machine we passed in the hallway," said Ning's mother. "Don't wander off, now, okay?"

"Okay, mom. I'm not a little kid, you know," Ning grumbled. Ning's mother smiled, gave her a quick kiss on the top of the head, and left. "Why are parents so embarrassing?" Ning muttered.

"Aw, I thought it was sweet," teased Marcus.

"I might just have one good arm," threatened Ning, "but I can still bop you with it."

"Are you nervous about having an X-ray examination?" Lucía asked.

"A little," Ning replied. "Does it hurt?"

"No, not at all," Zac said. He looked around the

waiting room. There were only a couple of people left, and they had just been called by a nurse. "I've got an idea," said Zac, "but we have to be quick." He pulled his phone out of his pocket.

"Who are we going to see?" asked Ning.

"A guy named Wilhelm Roentgen," Zac said (pronouncing it *REHNT guhn*). "He discovered X rays, so I bet he'll be able to tell us about them." The friends gathered in for a selfie, taking care not to bump Ning's arm. Zac hit the Backspace button.

FLASH!

ZUMMMMMMmmmmmmmm...

The friends were transported by virtual reality from the waiting room to a small, dark laboratory.

"This is Roentgen's laboratory, in 1895, and that is his X-ray machine." Zac pointed to a glass tube held over what looked like a picture frame. The tube looked a little like a long light bulb.

Suddenly, the door opened. A bearded man entered, followed closely by a woman. The man carried something covered in a cloth. The two were so busy arguing that they didn't notice the children.

"That's Roentgen and his wife, Anna," Zac explained. "They're German. I'll turn on the translation feature so you can understand what they're saying." Zac tapped the screen of his phone.

"I tell you, my dear, you will not believe what I am about to show you. It will change medicine forever," said Wilhelm. He pulled the cover away from the thing he was carrying. It was a photograph of a hand. ("Anna's hand," Zac whispered.) Inside the outline of the hand, the bones were clearly visible.

"That is the first ever X-ray image of the human body," said Zac. "Impressive, huh?"

Anna did not look impressed. She stared at the photograph, gasping at the skeletal hand. "I feel like I have seen my own death!" she exclaimed.

"No, not death!" her husband tried to comfort her.

"Instead, this will save lives! And do you know how?"

"By allowing doctors to look inside the body without surgery!" said Zac. Roentgen spun around, surprised by the noise. "Oh, sorry," said Zac. "I didn't mean to interrupt."

"No problem, my friend," laughed Roentgen. "You are right. X rays will allow us to see inside the body without cutting into it, risking the patient's health."

"Can you show us how it works?" asked Zac.

Roentgen pointed to the glass tube. "This tube produces a kind of invisible radiation called X rays," he explained. "The frame below holds photographic paper. My wife simply held her hand over the frame. X rays from the tube passed right through her flesh, producing an image of her bones on the photographic paper. You can even see her wedding ring!"

"Roentgen's invention took off quickly," Zac whispered to the other children. "By 1896, hospitals began setting up special departments to conduct X-ray examinations of their patients."

"Speaking of hospitals and X rays," said Lucía, "it might be time for Ning's."

"Good point," said Zac. He touched his phone, and Roentgen's lab disappeared—just in time, as a doctor came around the corner with Ning's mom.

"Hello, Ning," the doctor said. "I just wanted to answer any worries about the X ray you'll be having."

"It's okay. I'm not worried. I know how it works, so I'm not afraid," Ning replied.

"That's great to hear," the doctor replied. "The X rays will help us figure out what kind of fracture you have."

"Fracture?" said Ning.

"It's what we call breaks in bones," said the doctor. "You see, bones are really strong…" the doctor began.

"So, why did mine break?" asked Ning.

"Well, with enough force, even hard things like bones can break. The worst kind of break is a compound fracture—that's when the bone snaps completely and pushes out through the skin."

"Eeeewwwwwww," said Marcus, wincing.

"Luckily, you don't appear to have one of those," said the doctor. "I suspect you may have what we call a greenstick fracture. That happens when the bone bends and cracks, but doesn't break completely."

"I get it," said Marcus. "Greenstick, like a soft, green twig on a tree. It's easy to bend, but hard to break."

"That's right," the doctor continued. "Ning, your bones are still growing, so they're a bit softer and more flexible than an adult's bones. There's only one way to find out what kind of fracture for sure. Let's get you down to the radiology department for your X ray."

"See you later, Ning. Let us know how it goes," said Zac. The friends left Ning and her mother and headed out of the hospital.

"Oh, I'm glad we're leaving," said Lucía. "Hospitals always remind me of the time my grandma got sick when I was little. Every time I smell that hospital smell, it's like I'm right back there."

"Your memory is being triggered by your senses," said Zac. "The sense of smell is closely linked to memory."

"What do you mean?" asked Marcus.

"Let me explain…" said Zac.

Chapter 3

Making Sense(s)

The friends turned onto Zac's street. The house on the corner had flowers planted along the edge of the sidewalk.

"Now that's perfect," said Zac.

"What is? Mrs. Merino's front yard?" asked Marcus. "I didn't know you were a such a big fan of flowers."

"No," Zac laughed. "I mean they're perfect for explaining about senses. Go on, have a smell."

Marcus and Lucía leaned over and took a deep sniff.

"When you smell something," Zac explained, "you're actually sensing chemicals. Chemicals from the flower enter through your nose into a larger space called the nasal cavity."

"The top of the cavity has a lining called the olfactory epithelium. It's full of cells that can detect different chemicals. These cells are linked with the brain—the same part of the brain that deals with memories. Lucía,

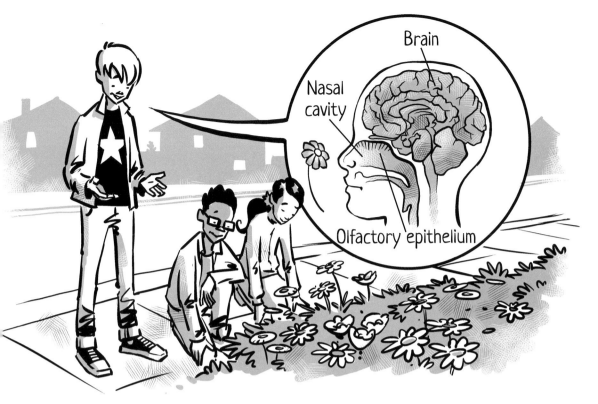

that is probably why the smell of the hospital triggers such strong memories in you."

"Oh, I see," said Lucía. "Hey look, it's Orbit!"

The dog came trotting down the block.

"Here, boy," said Zac. "Now, Orbit has a much better sense of smell than does any human—all dogs do. Even so, a person with a good sense of smell can detect around 10,000 different chemicals."

"Wow, that's a lot," said Marcus.

"And there's other cool stuff, too. Your sense of smell

can affect your sense of taste. Marcus, have you been enjoying your food much lately?"

"Not really. It doesn't taste like much. Even pepperoni pizza tastes bland, and that's my favorite."

"Yeah, it's weird, isn't it?" said Zac. "Your cold has your nose all stuffed up. Believe it or not, you need your sense of smell to help you taste stuff."

"Why is that?" asked Lucía.

"Well, your sense of taste is probably your least developed sense," said Zac. "It's pretty basic, really. Look, I'll show you."

Zac took out his phone. "I've been working on a magnification app. It uses the built-in camera to turn my phone into a portable microscope."

Zac turned on the app and stuck out his tongue. He held the phone over his mouth. The screen was filled with the image of something slimy and pink.

"Ew, what is that?" said Lucía.

"Ethth ma thunnn," said Zac.

"Excuse me?" said Marcus.

Zac popped his tongue back into his mouth. "I said, it's my tongue. Now this time, I want you to look for the bumps."

Zac held the cell phone over his tongue again. The camera focused. Dozens of little pink bumps appeared on the screen. "I see them!" said Lucía.

"They're called papillae," said Zac, pronouncing it *puh PIHL ee,* "but the more common name is taste buds. Not all taste buds detect the same taste. Some pick up sweet tastes, some sour, some salty, and some bitter. Some pick up a meaty taste called *umami.* Taste buds can only distinguish these five sensations. The rest of the flavor of food comes from what you smell. The two senses work together to produce the sensation of flavor."

"So, my blocked nose is stopping me from smelling

what I'm tasting," said Marcus.

"Who knew you needed your nose to taste stuff? Senses are weird," said Lucía.

"I'll tell you what else is weird—your eyes see stuff upside down," said Zac.

"What?" said Lucía and Marcus together.

"I'll show you," said Zac.

He tapped the screen on his phone and held the camera up to his eye. The phone projected into mid-air a three-dimensional image of the inside of Zac's eye.

"Cool..." said Lucía.

"More like weird," said Marcus.

"When you look at one of these flowers, what you are really seeing is the light reflecting off it. The light enters your eye through the pupil—the black spot in the middle. Behind the pupil, you have a lens,

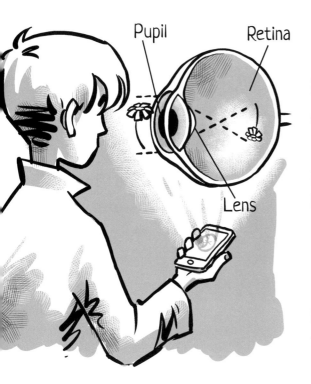

Pupil   Retina

Lens

kind of like the lens of a magnifying glass. The lens gathers the light, projecting it onto the back of the eye."

"But the image is upside down!" said Lucía, pointing to the back of the eye.

"The image falls onto the back of the eye, on a part called the retina," Zac continued. "The retina has millions of special cells that sense light and color. They send this information to the brain. The brain flips the image right-side up."

Zac reached down without looking and grabbed one of the flowers, stroking its petals.

"This brings us to the sense of touch. Your skin is full of different types of touch sensors. They can feel when something is pressing against you, or whether a surface is smooth or rough. The sensors send these messages to the brain."

"Zac Newton, I hope you're not damaging those flowers!" came a shout from the house.

"Sorry, Mrs. Merino!" Zac called back.

"How did she even know we were here?" said Lucía.

"She probably heard us," said Marcus. "Which, I believe, is the last of the senses."

"Yes and no," said Zac. He fished a piece of chalk from his pocket and started doodling on the sidewalk.

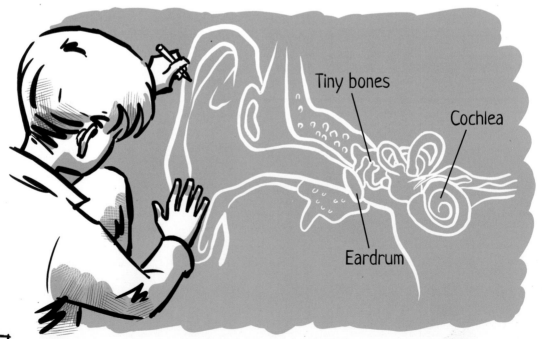

Tiny bones

Cochlea

Eardrum

"What's that you're drawing?" asked Marcus. "A maze?"

"No, it's the inside of your ear. Sound is really just the result of vibrations, or movements, in the air. These vibrations enter the ear and travel here, to your eardrum."

Zac pointed out the parts of the ear as he spoke.

"The eardrum vibrates against the smallest bones in the body. These bones pass on the vibrations to the cochlea—that's pronounced *KOK lee uh.*"

"That's the swirly part?" asked Lucía.

"That's right. The cochlea is filled with fluid. The vibrations are transferred to the fluid. Also inside the cochlea, there are hairs that can pick up vibrations in the fluid. They turn the vibrations into nerve signals, which are sent to the brain."

"Zac Newton!" Mrs. Merino's voice startled them again. "Is that you drawing on my sidewalk?"

"Don't worry, I'm erasing it, Mrs. Merino," Zac replied. He scuffed at the drawing with his sneaker.

"When I said hearing was the last sense, you said *yes and no*. What did you mean by that?" asked Marcus.

"Well, we have more senses than just those five," Zac replied. "For example, when I reached down to grab that flower, how did I know how far to reach without looking? That's part of my sense of spatial awareness. There are special sensors in the body that help me know the position of my arm, so I know how far I'm reaching. And Ning's sense of balance helps with her gymnastics. Scientists don't agree on exactly how many senses we have, but it's certainly more than five."

"A..a..a...achooo!" Marcus let out a huge sneeze. "Well, with this cold of mine, I have one less sense than the rest of you. I can't smell anything!"

Chapter 4
Surfing the Bloodstream

"Could you get all those sneezes out before we go inside?" asked Lucía as the children returned to Zac's house.

"Sorry, I can't help it," Marcus answered. "I think my body is broken."

"Broken? Not at all!" exclaimed Zac. "Your body is working the way it's supposed to."

"It doesn't feel like it," said Marcus.

"No, I bet it doesn't. But when you sneeze, that's your body trying to get rid of germs. That's your immune system at work," Zac explained.

"Say what, now?" said Marcus.

The friends entered through the back door and marched downstairs, returning to the basement. Marcus and Lucía plopped down on the old couch.

Zac began to explain, "Your immune system has the job of keeping bad things out of your body, like viruses and bacteria. We call them germs. They're tiny living things that can get inside your body and multiply and make you sick. When you sneeze, that's your body trying to get rid of germs."

"I've heard that sudden, bright light can also make some people sneeze," said Lucía.

"It's true," said Zac, "although nobody really knows why."

"But, back to the immune system," said Zac. "It is working all the time to protect you. Most of the time, you don't even notice. Think of your body as a castle. Your immune system is made up of all the castle's defenses. Together, it's their job to keep out invaders."

Zac reached into a nearby box labeled "old kitchen stuff." He pulled out a pot lid and held it like a shield. In the other hand, he brandished a wooden spoon, facing off against an imaginary army of invading germs.

"For example, your nose is lined with hairs that trap

germs on the way in."

"You should see my grandpa's nose hair," said Marcus. "He must be super protected."

Zac laughed. "Then there's your skin. Your skin doesn't just keep all your insides on the inside. It also keeps everything else out. It's like the castle walls, keeping out all those germ invaders." He thumped the spoon against his pot-lid shield.

"Well, you're not going to keep me out," called a voice from the top of the stairs.

"Ning!" cried the friends. Ning came down the stairs. Her arm was held to her side in a sling. The friends could see her wrist was wrapped in a stiff cast.

"The good news," Ning said, "is that I just have a

greenstick fracture in my wrist. The bad news is that I have to keep this cast on for six weeks! That means no sports, no excitement, no nothing."

"Oh, Ning, I'm sorry," said Lucía.

"It wasn't your fault," said Ning. "I should have been more careful." Orbit rubbed his head against her leg. He let out a whimper of apology. "You're okay, Orbit." Ning petted him with her good arm. "It's not your fault, either."

"I think I can do something about the lack of excitement," said Zac.

"Really?" said Ning, perking up.

"Yeah! We've been talking about the immune system," Zac replied.

"Oh. Sounds… thrilling," said Ning sarcastically.

"Trust me," said Zac, taking out his cell phone. "This will be like the best theme park ride ever."

The friends gathered together.

FLASH!

ZUMMMMMMmmmmmmm...

When the flash faded, the friends were swirling down a large tube. They were surrounded by rushing liquid. Strange-looking objects floated all around them.

"Where are we?" shouted Ning.

"And how come we can speak underwater?" said Lucía.

"Remember, this is virtual reality." Zac laughed. "In real life, it would be dark in here. And we're not underwater—we're in a blood vessel, surrounded by plasma."

"Plasma?" said Ning.

"Plasma is the liquid part of the blood. It helps to move blood cells around the body. It also carries nutrients—food for the cells of the body. The plasma delivers nutrients to the cells and carries away their wastes."

"And what are those disks?" asked Lucía. She pointed to a flattened blob nearly as big as she. It was bright red, and it looked kind of like a donut without a hole.

"Those are red blood cells," Zac explained. "They carry oxygen all around the body. All the cells in the body need oxygen, so red blood cells are important. Those other ones, they're white blood cells." He pointed to a cell that was round and covered in bumps.

"It looks almost like a giant snowball!" said Marcus.

Zac continued, "White blood cells are the ones that attack any germs that get into your body. They are the soldiers of the immune system."

Zac climbed on top of a red blood cell. "Now, how about a bit of surfing?" he said, waving his arms to steady himself.

"Yes!" shouted Ning, mounting another blood cell.

The friends swirled through the blood vessel, taking in the weird sights.

"Why's Orbit's surfboard so much darker than yours?" asked Marcus.

The friends noticed that Orbit's cell had a darker, almost purplish color.

"Red blood cells get their color from the oxygen they carry. Orbit's cell must have already delivered its oxygen," said Zac. "It'll get reloaded with more oxygen when it reaches the lungs."

"So, where will this take us?" asked Lucía.

"The blood is pumped around the body by the heart," Zac explained. "It sends blood to the lungs to get oxygen. Then, it sends the oxygen-filled blood around the body."

The kids spotted a strange cell ahead that didn't look like the others. Several of the snowball-like cells had surrounded it. "What's that?" asked Lucía.

"That's a germ. And those white blood cells are attacking it," said Zac. "As you can see, the white cells are struggling right now. But once they've determined how to defeat it, they can share this ability with other immune cells. If the body meets a similar germ in the future, the immune cells will 'remember' how to deal with it."

"The immune system rocks!" said Marcus. "It can deal with anything!"

"Sometimes, it needs a little help," said Zac. "Watch this."

FLASH!

ZUMMMMMMMmmmmmmmm...

"Hey, where did the ride go?" asked Ning.

The children were now in a room with wood-paneled walls. A young boy and his mother stood in front of a man in a dark suit, who was handling some tubes.

"We're in England, in 1796," said Zac. "The man over there is Edward Jenner, a doctor. Jenner is about to do something pretty daring to that kid."

The friends watched Jenner scrape the boy's arm with a sharp metal instrument.

"What's he doing?" asked Lucía.

"Jenner has just put a disease called smallpox into the boy's bloodstream. It's a deadly disease that used to kill millions of people."

"What!" cried Lucía. "Stop him!"

The man looked up from his work. "I understand your concern, but don't be alarmed," he said. "The boy will be fine, because I inoculated him earlier."

"You did what?" asked Marcus.

"Inoculated him," Jenner continued. "I gave him the cure before he even got the disease. You see, I've noticed that milkmaids never get smallpox. But they do catch a similar disease, called cowpox, from the cows they milk."

"And what does cowpox do?" asked Ning.

"It's not too bad—just a bit of a fever. The milkmaids recover easily. But afterward, they don't catch smallpox."

"Remember those white blood cells we saw fighting that germ?" Zac reminded his friends. "They were having a tough time. But once they 'learn' how to defeat the germ, the body becomes immune to it. Cowpox and smallpox are very similar. So, once the body 'learns' how to fight cowpox, it also becomes immune to smallpox."

"So, did you give the boy cowpox?" asked Lucía.

"Yes, I gave James here cowpox a few days ago. Now, I'm proving my theory by trying to give him smallpox. Of course, he will not catch the disease, because he is immune."

"Amazing!" said Ning.

"In fact, it was such an amazing discovery that no one quite believed it," whispered Zac to the others. "Jenner was forced to repeat the experiment, to prove he was totally sure what he was doing. He even tried it on his own son!"

"Sounds dangerous," said Lucía.

"Things were different back then." Zac explained. "There weren't the same rules and regulations as there are today."

Zac continued, "Jenner took a risk. But he had not only prevented smallpox. He had invented inoculation. That means injecting something into a person to make the body immune to a disease. Remember those shots we got before school started?"

"Yes," said Lucía. She rubbed her arm as if she could still feel the needle's sting.

"Those were inoculations," Zac explained. "Today, we're inoculated against tons of diseases that used to kill millions of children."

"I think I preferred surfing on blood cells," said Ning.

"Okay!" Zac laughed. "We'll go back!"

Chapter 5
Brilliant Brains

With the tap of Zac's phone screen, the scene shifted in front of the friends' eyes. They were once again traveling through a blood vessel.

"So, are we going to the heart?" asked Lucía.

"No, I've skipped that part. I thought we'd take a trip to the brain instead," Zac replied.

"Blood goes to the brain?" said Marcus.

"Oh, yeah! In fact, the brain needs more blood flow than any other part of your body," said Zac.

"Why does the brain need so much blood?" asked Lucía.

"It's because the brain uses so much oxygen and nutrients," said Zac. "Brains are like miniature supercomputers. They use a lot of energy."

"Even yours, Marcus," giggled Ning.

"We should be getting close now," said Zac. "The brain lies just beyond the walls of these blood vessels."

"Whoa!" shouted Lucía. "What's happening?" The children watched as the cells that made up the lining of the blood vessel packed closer and closer together. Before, nutrients, large molecules, and even some cells had been able to pass through the vessel walls with ease. Now, the cells were packed so tightly that only the smallest molecules and nutrients could get through.

"Ah, we've reached the blood-brain barrier!" said Zac. "It's like the brain's own security fence. It helps to protect the brain from germs and other dangerous things. It only lets through water, oxygen, nutrients, and a few other things the brain needs."

"That's pretty cool," said Marcus. "But it doesn't look like we'll be able to pass through!"

"Maybe this isn't the best way to see the brain," said Zac. He tapped some buttons on his phone, and the friends were standing in an empty room. A giant, virtual brain hovered above them.

"I never realized it was so slimy-looking!" said Ning.

"It looks like a cauliflower," said Lucía.

"If you eat cauliflowers that look like that, remind me never to have dinner at your house," said Marcus.

"It might look like a vegetable, but the brain is the most amazing part of your body," said Zac. "It's made up over 100 billion nerve cells. It uses up about a fifth of your body's energy."

"But it's not very big," said Marcus.

"Speak for yourself," said Ning.

Marcus made a face at her. "What I mean is, it only

weighs a few pounds, or just over a kilogram. How come it uses so much energy?"

"Well, for one thing, it does so much," Zac explained. "Your brain signals your muscles to make you move. It stores your memories. It triggers your emotions. It provides your imagination, gathers information from the senses…"

"Yeah, I suppose," said Marcus.

"It controls your breathing and keeps your heart pumping. It allows you to speak, to solve problems, and to learn how to do things," Zac continued.

"Okay, we get it!" said Ning.

"In short, your brain is what makes you... you. When I think that we have something like that inside us, it kind of blows my mind," said Zac.

"Hold on a second," said Ning, walking around the hovering image. "Is this just one brain? It looks like two glued together."

"Yes, it's one brain, but you're right that it has two

halves. Each one is called a hemisphere. And each hemisphere has different things to do—different functions. Oddly, each side of the brain controls certain functions on the opposite side of the body."

"So, the right half of my body is being controlled by the left half of my brain?" said Ning.

"Yep. Each half seems to have other specialized functions as well. Many of the parts that deal with language and mathematics are in the left half. Some functions, like creativity, make more use of the right half. But most tasks involve many different areas on both sides of the brain."

"I'm guessing that your brain is bigger on the left side, Zac," joked Marcus.

"If you look closely, you'll see it's split into more than just two halves. There are different areas, too," said Zac, pointing to the parts of the brain.

"Each area does a different job. The biggest part, there at the top, is the cerebrum—*suh REE bruhm*. It controls thoughts and many kinds of learning. It also handles information from the senses and some kinds

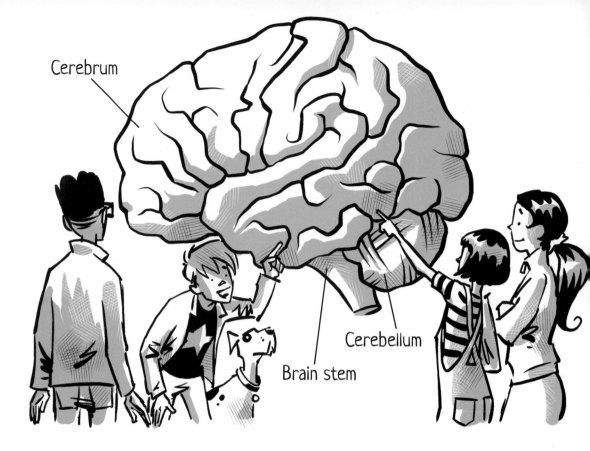

Cerebrum

Cerebellum

Brain stem

of movements. Lots of cool things happen up there."

"What's that part?" asked Lucía. "The smaller part underneath."

"That's called the cerebellum—*sehr uh BEHL um*—and it controls balance, posture, and coordination," Zac continued. "The cerebellum handles many of the movements that we have learned to do without thinking, like walking. The more we practice something, the better the cerebellum gets at telling the body how to do it."

"That's how I got good at cartwheels," said Ning.

"Not with dogs around," said Marcus.

"Lucía can't do cartwheels yet," explained Zac, "but the more she works at it, the easier the cerebellum will find it to control her movements."

Zac crouched by the model and pointed to the smallest part. "This long, thin piece of the brain is called the brain stem. This does a lot of things that you think come naturally, like breathing. Without signals from this part of your brain, you'd die."

"Wow, if my brain is so important, maybe I should wear a helmet all the time," joked Marcus.

"Well, you kind of have one built in," said Zac. "Your skull is there to protect your brain from any bumps. The brain is also floating in a fluid that cushions it from damage. Of course, you may need to wear a helmet as well, depending on what you're doing. Your skull wasn't built for falling off bicycles or getting hit by a baseball."

"Maybe I'll wear one when I try cartwheels next

time," joked Lucía.

"All this thinking about thinking is hard work. To be honest, it's making me hungry," Marcus complained. His stomach grumbled in agreement.

"Yeah, I'm hungry too," said Zac. "Let's eat." The virtual brain disappeared, and the friends were back in Zac's basement. "Anyone want anything in particular?"

"Anything but cauliflower," said Marcus.

Chapter 6
Down the Hatch

When the children had finished their snack, Zac loaded the dirty plates into the dishwasher. He insisted on doing it himself. "I always load it in the most efficient way," he bragged.

"You know, Zac, for a cool guy, you can sometimes sound like a massive nerd," said Marcus.

"Hey, there are plenty of cool nerds!" Zac laughed. "Eating a sandwich hasn't cheered you up, has it?"

"No, that's just Marcus," sighed Ning. She gave him a playful poke on the arm.

"Eating my sandwich got me thinking," said Lucía. "How does my body turn something like that into the stuff I need to live?"

"How about a journey to find out?" asked Zac.

"Like the blood cell ride?" said Ning.

"Oh, even better!" said Zac. "Selfie time!"

FLASH!

ZUMMMMMMmmmmmmm...

When the light faded, the friends were inside what looked to be some kind of cave. The floor squished and bounced beneath their feet, like an inflatable rubber pillow.

"Zac, why is everything you show us so slimy?" said Ning.

"Hold on, I recognize these bumps," said Lucía, eyeing the floor with suspicion. "Are these taste buds?"

"You are correct!" said Zac. "We're standing on the tongue. And that gloopy lump of stuff over there is a bolus—a ball of chewed up food. Inside the mouth, everything's damp with saliva. All the spit makes it easier to swallow."

"Zac, you take us to the nicest places," said Marcus.

The tongue began to move beneath them. "Get ready," said Zac, "we're going down!"

With a sudden jerk, the tongue flexed. It pushed the bolus and the friends to the back of the mouth. Then they were gone, tumbling through a large hole.

"Whooooaaahhh!" shouted Zac, waving his arms over his head. "This is the esophagus—a tube that goes down your neck."

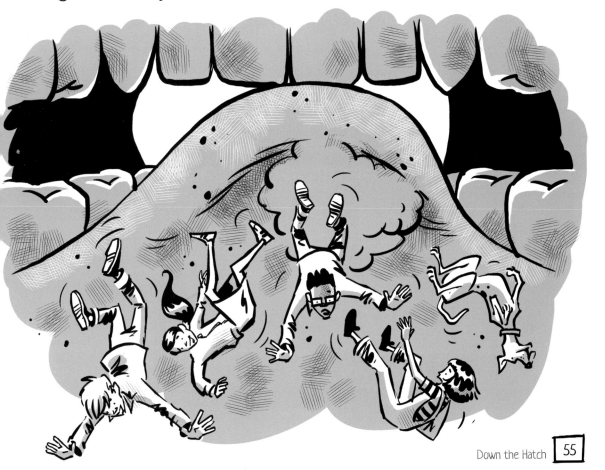

"The walls are moving in and out," said Lucía.

"Yes, the esophagus walls have muscles that help to push the food downward," Zac explained. "This part's pretty quick. We'll be splashing down in four...three... two..."

"Splashing down?" said Marcus. "Wh...."

Before Marcus could finish, the friends were squeezed out of the esophagus along with the bolus. They landed in a pool of slimy liquid.

"One!" shouted Zac. "Welcome to the stomach."

"I've been slimed!" said Lucía. "This is disgusting!"

Zac roared with laughter at the sight of his friends covered in the goopy mess. "Oh, it's worse than slime. It's chewed up food and stomach juices."

"That's really disgusting!" Marcus complained.

"The stomach juices include a kind of acid that helps to break down the food," Zac explained.

"Let's get out of here!" said Ning.

"That's probably a good idea," Zac said. "Food normally stays in the stomach for a few hours. By then, it's broken down enough to move on. Hanging around that long would be boring, though. Let's head for the opening at the bottom of the stomach."

"If that's the way out, I'll take it," said Marcus.

"By the time the food reaches this point, it's been mushed into a thick liquid called chyme" said Zac, pronouncing it *kym*. "Now, get ready—things are about to get tight."

The friends were pushed out of the stomach and into a narrow tube.

"This is the small intestine," Zac explained. "It's narrow, but it's really long. The small intestine is actually around 20 feet long, or 6 meters. It has to wind back and forth just to fit inside the body."

The walls were covered in millions of little stalks

that looked like fingers. "What are these for?" asked Marcus.

"They're called villi," Zac answered. "It's their job to absorb useful chemicals from the chime. The chemicals travel through the blood stream to the liver. The liver turns them into stored energy and other useful things that can be sent throughout the body. But, we're not going to the liver. Let's follow what's left of the chime into the large intestine."

"Let me guess, the large intestine is bigger than the small intestine," said Marcus.

"It's wider, that's true." Zac smiled. "But it is also shorter. This is where the leftovers of digestion collect—things that have had all their nutrients absorbed or are too difficult to break down."

"The walls are moving here, too," said Lucía. "Is that the large intestine pushing everything along?"

"Yes, in part. The intestine is also squeezing the leftovers to absorb any extra water."

"It's starting to look like…" said Marcus.

"That's exactly what it is…" said Zac, cutting him off. Zac tried to think of a polite word to use. "Waste," he finally decided. "Solid waste, ready to leave the body. What doctors call *feces*. For this stuff, the next stop is the bathroom…"

"I think we've come far enough for the moment," Lucía interrupted.

"I agree," said Zac, chuckling. He pressed a button on his phone, and the children left the large intestine far behind.

Chapter 7

Flex Those Muscles

Back in the basement, Ning said, "Thanks, Zac. That journey into the body was awesome!"

"Yeah, the Backspace app is amazing! How did you do it?" asked Lucía.

"Well," Zac answered, "Usually it just shows us events in history. But I've changed it by adding information about the body. It uses lots of images from the web. The better the images, the more realistic the virtual world looks. These days, it's easy for us to see how the body works. We can scan the body with X rays…"

"I know all about them," Ning reminded him.

"Of course." Zac continued, "There are also other kinds of scans, besides X rays, and devices called probes that can be used to see inside the body. We've never known so much about how the body works."

"It must have been different hundreds of years ago," said Marcus. "I bet they had to guess what was wrong with sick people or how all parts of the body work together."

"Yes and no," said Zac. "Some people were way ahead of their time. But instead of telling you about it, I'll take you to meet someone. Come on, you know the routine."

The children gathered together.

"Get ready for the 1500's," said Zac

"You coming, Orbit?" said Ning.

The dog looked back at her doubtfully.

"Come on, boy. No hard feelings."

Orbit trotted over and joined the group.

FLASH!

ZUMMMMMMmmmmmmm...

The room that took form around them was uncomfortably stuffy. The windows were shuttered against bright daylight, which glinted here and there through the cracks. Inside, candles blazed around a table and a drawing easel. The children arrived just as two men carried a stretcher draped with cloth out of the room. An older, bearded man was inspecting the drawing on the easel.

"I'd better turn on the translation function," said Zac. "There's going to be a bit of Italian in a moment. We're going to talk to Leonardo da Vinci."

"What is that smell?" hissed Ning.

The man at the easel looked up. "Ah, my friends, welcome, welcome," he said. "If you were here earlier, you could have joined me. Come and see."

He waved them over to the easel. It held an incredibly detailed sketch of the muscles inside a human leg.

"Wow, that's an amazing drawing," said Lucía.

"And it's incredibly accurate," Zac whispered to his friends. "Leonardo was hundreds of years ahead of his time. No one was doing drawings like this."

"Look closely, and you can see how the muscles work," Leonardo encouraged. "The muscles work by contracting, or tightening. See how their ends are attached to the bones?" He pointed. "When the muscles contract, they pull on the bones. If the

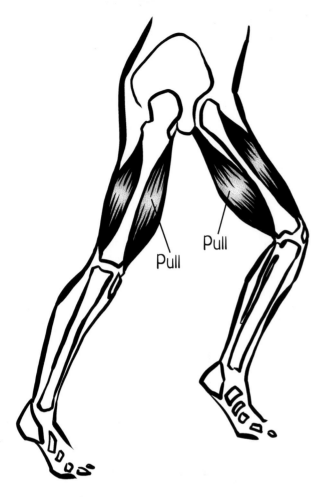

Pull

Pull

muscles on the top of the thigh contract, they pull on the front of the leg, straightening the knee. When the muscles underneath the thigh contract, they pull on the back of the leg, and the knee bends. Always pulling, never pushing."

"So, when you straighten your front leg for a cartwheel," said Ning, pointing to the sketch, "it must be the muscle on top of the thigh that does the pulling."

"You have to straighten your front leg?" asked Lucía. "I think I just figured out what I was doing wrong…"

"Ah, we have some gymnasts as well as scientists, I see," said Leonardo.

"Now look at this…" Leonardo started digging through a pile of papers.

"There are different types of muscle," Zac explained to the children as they waited. "Skeletal muscles, like the ones Leonardo was drawing, are attached to bones. They help us move. Smooth muscle is what we saw pushing things along in the digestive system. The last type, called cardiac muscle, is used by the heart to pump blood around the body."

Leonardo returned holding another sketch.

"When I think about my drawings, I think not only as an artist but as an engineer. The wonders of the body are not so different from the wonders of nature and the works of people. See here: the lungs are connected to the mouth and nose by tubes—like a river flowing into a lake. And here, the blood vessels from the heart connect to the lungs, just as canals connect the various parts of Venice. It is so complex and yet so beautiful."

"How do you get the drawings to look so lifelike?" Lucía asked.

"Well, if you had been here earlier, you would have seen the body I was using," Leonardo answered.

"A real body?" asked Ning.

"Yes, of course," said Leonardo. "You seem shocked. Don't worry, the person was already dead before I started my work…"

"Was that what was on that stretcher when we came in?" asked Marcus.

"Yes, yes, that was the one. It is difficult to work in this heat, as the bodies start to smell. I close the shutters to keep the heat out, but…" Leonardo shrugged. "I'm lucky to get the bodies at all. Sometimes I have to use animals to practice instead."

Even Orbit looked alarmed by that.

"I think that animals and people are very similar on the inside. When I can't find a human model for what I need to draw, I use my knowledge of animals and make a good guess at how it looks in humans."

"I don't feel very well," said Ning. She was starting to look pale.

"Thank you, Master Leonardo," said Zac said quickly, "but we must be going."

"A pity, I could have shown you my other drawings." Leonardo swept his arm over a pile of papers on his desk.

"Maybe another time," said Zac. He switched off the app, and the scene disappeared.

"Cutting apart dead bodies and animals, how awful!" said Ning.

"In Leonardo's time," Zac explained, "they didn't have X rays to look inside the body. Cutting apart dead bodies was often the only way to figure out how the body works. Besides, the work of Leonardo and others helped lead to the development of modern medicine, which has saved millions of lives."

"I guess so," said Ning. "But if it's all the same, I'd rather learn about the body using X rays."

Chapter 8

Tiny Monsters

Orbit padded across Zac's basement and laid down in his dog bed. He gave himself a vigorous scratch with his hind leg. He looked happy.

"Hey, Zac, I hope your dog doesn't have fleas," said Marcus.

"We try to watch out for that, but you never know," Zac answered. "Anyway, he wouldn't be the only one in this house with animals living on him."

"What are you saying? I don't have fleas!" Marcus protested.

"Maybe not fleas, but tiny creatures you can't even see," Zac explained. "It's not just you, either. It's all of us. Some of them we need to be healthy. Look, I'll show you with my microscope. Actually, no, let's start with a quick trip to the 1600's. There's a man we should meet first."

"He's not going to be cutting up bodies, is he?" said Ning, holding her stomach. "I'm just now feeling better."

"No dead people—I promise," said Zac. "All right, gather up. Make sure I can see you all in the screen. Orbit, are you coming?"

Orbit raised an eyebrow in suspicion.

"Guess not, then. Well, here goes…"

FLASH!

ZUMMMMMMmmmmmmmm...

Where Orbit had been lying not a second before, there sat a man. He wore a long, curled wig and a long coat. He was perched at a large desk.

"Good morning, and welcome to the beautiful city of Delft," said the man. ("That's in the Netherlands," Zac whispered to the others, "in northwestern Europe.") "How may I be of assistance?" the man continued.

"Mister Leeuwenhoek," Zac began (pronouncing it *LAY vuhn hook),* "I was wondering, could you show us some of your discoveries?" Zac asked.

"But of course!" The man waved them over to his desk. "These papers have just been published." He spread pages of drawings across the desk. They showed a variety of objects that looked like worms and seed pods.

"These are the tiny creatures I have discovered. I call them *animalcules.* They are completely invisible to the naked eye."

"These drawings are amazingly detailed," gasped Zac. He turned to his friends, "*Animalcules* is the name Anton van Leeuwenhoek gave to the tiny living things that he discovered, including bacteria."

"What are bacteria?" whispered Ning.

"They're among the simplest forms of life," Zac explained. "They're made up of a single tiny cell."

"I've heard bacteria can be dangerous," said Marcus, "but I never knew they were so small."

"You're right, some bacteria can make you sick," said Zac. "But not all of them are harmful. Some are even helpful. For example, bacteria in our digestive system help us to break down our food."

"If these animalcules are so small, how did you see them?" Lucía asked the scientist.

"With this," Leeuwenhoek replied. He held up a small, flat piece of metal with a large screw at the bottom and a tiny drop of glass at the top. "This is the microscope. I invented this one myself. It is five times more powerful than any other microscope in the world!"

"Thanks for showing us your work,
Mr. Leeuwenhoek," said Zac, "but we have to go now."

Leeuwenhoek waved goodbye. Zac tapped the screen of his cell phone. In an instant, the scene disappeared, and they were surrounded by the modern day again. Where the scientist had been, Orbit was lying in his bed.

"You know, I kind of think Orbit would look good in one of those fancy wigs," said Marcus. "We might even change his name to Leeuwenhoek!"

Lucía paid him no attention. Instead, she questioned Zac. "So, when you were talking about people having tiny creatures on them, you meant bacteria?"

"Not quite. I took you to meet Leeuwenhoek to show that living things can look different than you might expect. Let me show you what I was really thinking of..."

Zac held up his arm to take the selfie. "Oh, I see

you're coming this time, Orbit. Afraid of missing out?"

FLASH!

ZUMMMMMMmmmmmmm...

A weird landscape stretched around them. The ground was bumpy and dry. It might have looked like a desert, except there were so many trees. They were strange-looking trees, too. They had no branches or leaves. They simply narrowed as they stretched into the sky.

"Where are we?" said Marcus.

"This is what the surface of human face looks like close up," Zac replied.

"You're kidding!" said Lucía.

"So, what are these?" asked Ning, wandering up to one of the trees. It was so wide that she couldn't get her arms around it.

"Those are eyelashes," Zac replied. "And those flat things on the ground are flakes of dead skin."

Suddenly, Orbit started barking furiously and running around them in circles.

"What is it, Orbit?" Ning asked.

From behind one of the hairs walked a monster. It had eight chunky legs on the front of its body and a long, thick tail. Numerous eyes peered out on either side of its head.

"Aaaarrrgghhh!" screamed Ning, Lucía, and Marcus.

Zac calmly walked toward the beast.

"Zac, run!" screamed Lucía.

"It's fine," Zac laughed. "Like I said before, this is just virtual reality." He scrambled onto the back of the monster.

"Zac!" shouted Lucía.

"Don't worry," Zac reassured them. "This is *Demodex*

folliculorum, but we might call it the eyelash mite. It may look like something from a nightmare, but it's harmless. It mainly feeds on dead skin."

Orbit gave the mite a wary sniff.

"Tell me these things are not on my skin right now!" said Lucía.

"You might have a couple," said Zac. "People tend to get more as they get older. No one knows why, really. Old people usually have the most."

"I'm never hugging my grandma again," said Marcus.

"You have to remember, these critters are tiny, too," said Zac. "You can't even see them with your naked eye, or feel that they're there."

"Well, if they're the only animals on my skin…" said Lucía, wary.

"Oh, no, there are plenty of different kinds," said Zac cheerfully. "Head lice, dust mites…"

"Dude, you're not helping," said Marcus.

"Oh, well, in that case, let's say goodbye to my ride."

Zac slipped off the back of the mite and tapped the screen of his phone, and the terrifying beast was gone.

Chapter 9

DNA

"Speaking of bugs, something has been bugging me," said Lucía. "Da Vinci said he studied animals to help him guess what humans are like inside. It made me think, are we really that similar? I mean, what makes me me and not, for example, a dog? Dogs have skin and a heart, just like we do. So, what's the difference between me and, say, Orbit?"

"Well, Orbit's nicer," said Marcus. "And he's cuter. And he's funnier…"

"Ha ha, very funny," Lucía snapped. "But you know what I mean, Zac, don't you?"

"Well, humans and other animals are very similar and very different," Zac replied. "When da Vinci tried looking at animals to learn more about humans, he made mistakes. That's because we're different. But at the same time, we are alike. It all comes down to what's inside our cells. It's a little tough to explain…"

"Oh, great," Marcus muttered. "And I was worried it was going to be really simple."

"...but I know just the people who can help us."

FLASH!

ZUMMMMMMmmmmmmmm...

The basement transformed into a laboratory. The equipment looked pretty modern, but not totally up-to-date. There were no computers, but the children saw test tubes and beakers. Four scientists stood around a bench, looking at a colorful plastic model.

"This lab looks a little old because this is the 1950's," Zac explained. "Those people over there are Rosalind Franklin, Maurice Wilkins, Francis Crick, and James Watson. Together, they discovered the structure of DNA."

"DNA? What's that?" asked Ning.

"I know! I know!" said Marcus, excited. "They made dinosaurs out of it in that movie. It's like this... stuff that tells you how to make things."

"Well, I admire your enthusiasm, young man," Wilkins interrupted, "but perhaps I could help to explain. You are correct. DNA is a little bit like a long list of instructions. Only these instructions are 'written' in a kind of code. There's a copy of the code in each of the trillions of cells in your body. The DNA contains instructions that tell the cells how to develop and how to function."

"Kind of like computer code?" asked Lucía.

"A little bit, yes" said Zac.

Wilkins continued. "Your DNA helps to determine how your body grows and develops—and so, what you end up like. You get your DNA from your parents. Part of it comes from your mother, and part of it comes from your father. That is why people tend to look like their parents. Your DNA is a combination of their DNA."

"Can you just look at person's DNA?" Marcus asked.

"Not directly," Franklin said. "I noticed that one of you has a broken arm. I bet the hospital gave you an X-ray examination."

Ning nodded.

"Well," Franklin continued, "I used a kind of X-ray test to help figure out what DNA looks like. I wasn't able to see the structure directly. It's too tiny. But the way the X rays bounced off it helped me to figure out its shape."

Crick pointed at the model. "As you can see, DNA is shaped like a ladder, but one that has been twisted. We call this shape a *double helix*. The interesting part is not the sides of the ladder but the rungs."

"Each rung is made up of a pair of chemical units, called bases," said Watson, taking up the story. "There are four different bases in DNA, called adenine, thymine, cytosine, and guanine. Their order on the ladder makes up the code."

"This simple structure is the same for all living things. They all have this ladder, with rungs made up of the same four bases," said Wilkins.

"What's more," added Zac, "all living things share much of the same code. The more closely related two things are, the more similar their DNA is. So, for example,

humans and chimpanzees share about 96 percent of our DNA. We even share around 84 percent of our DNA with dogs. So, we are pretty similar to Orbit, after all."

"Ning likes running around and catching Frisbees," said Marcus, "I think she may have slightly more dog DNA than the rest of us."

"I swear, Marcus, if I didn't have this cast on my arm I'd…" said Ning.

"And on that note, I think it's time we left our brilliant scientists," said Zac. He tapped the screen of his cell phone, and the friends returned to the basement.

Chapter 10
Dr. Frankenstein

Marcus slouched in one of the basement chairs, looking glum. "My head hurts," he complained.

"Because of your cold?" asked Zac.

"No, I think I have information overload," said Marcus. "And, I'm still no closer to figuring out my science project."

"Hey, if this is going to turn into homework club, I'm going to go practice my cartwheels," said Lucía. "Ning, do you want to coach me? Let's leave Orbit behind this time."

The girls headed outside, leaving the boys and the dog downstairs.

"I have an idea," said Zac. "Why don't you make a human being?"

"What? Like Dr. Frankenstein? I think I can see some problems with that," replied Marcus. "But hold on a minute," he added, cheering up. "If we make another me, it could go to school, and I could stay in bed. Zac, I think you might be on to something here."

"No, not like that," said Zac. "I mean gather the chemical elements that make up your body. Think of the human body as a cake. What are the cake's ingredients?"

"So, people are made of chemical elements," said Marcus, thinking out loud.

"That's right, the simplest chemicals there are. Like… ah, there's one right away."

Zac bent down and picked up a nail.

"Here you go—iron. There's a tiny amount of iron in the human body. Red blood cells use iron to help them carry oxygen. That's one ingredient!"

"Oh, I see!" said Marcus.

"We just look for things with the right elements. Great. How many elements are there in a human body?"

"Only a handful of elements make up most of the body," Zac replied. "Then there's traces of other stuff. We should be able to get most of it."

"So, what are we waiting for? Let's get cracking," said Marcus.

"Okay, the most common element in the human body is oxygen," said Zac.

"Right, let's get some oxygen," said Marcus. "Wait! How do we get oxygen? Can we use a bottle of air?"

"Air is a mixture of lots of stuff," Zac explained, "not just oxygen. In fact, there's more nitrogen than oxygen. But there's also carbon dioxide and argon and…"

"Okay, I get it," said Marcus. "So, what do we do?"

"Well, most of the oxygen in your body is in the form of water. Grab a bottle of water, Marcus. Water is made up of oxygen and hydrogen, so that will also count for the body's hydrogen."

"Killing two birds with one stone?" Marcus teased. "Zac! You're finally starting to speak my language!"

"Right, what else do we need?" said Zac. "Carbon is next after oxygen."

"We could use a pencil lead for that," said Marcus.

"Right!" Zac agreed. "After oxygen, carbon, and hydrogen, the next most common element is nitrogen. Hold on... there's nitrogen in fertilizer. My mom keeps a jar of it under the kitchen sink for the houseplants."

"Great, that's nitrogen taken care of, thanks to Mrs. N. Now what?" asked Marcus.

"Calcium and phosphorus," Zac replied. "Phosphorus is easy. There's phosphorus in fertilizer, too." He ran off to the kitchen to grab a small sample of fertilizer. When he returned, he didn't look happy.

"I've been thinking, we might not be able to do this," Zac said.

"Why? Your mom wouldn't give you any fertilizer?" asked Marcus.

"No, not that." Zac explained, "I just don't think we'll be able to get all the elements we need. Not in their pure form, anyway. Take this fertilizer, for example. It's not just phosphorus and nitrogen. And how do we get potassium?"

"Easy! We learned in health class that there's potassium in bananas," said Marcus.

"Yes, but bananas aren't just potassium, are they? We can't really say that we're made of bananas."

"Zac, we're not trying to make a real person. It's my science project. We can get a little creative, as long as I can show my teacher that I learned something," said Marcus.

"Okay," replied Zac. "But if we're going to do it, let's do it as well as we can. There's more potassium in a sweet potato than in a banana, so let's use that. We'll also need sodium—table salt will do for that. There's chlorine… you have a swimming pool, don't you Marcus? There'll be chlorine in your pool cleaner."

Zac began to pace, still thinking out loud. "Calcium we can get from a piece of chalk. That leaves us with a whole list of things that we only have a tiny bit

of in our bodies: sulfur, magnesium, fluorine, zinc, silicon, aluminum, copper, iodine…"

"That's a lot of stuff," said Marcus. "We have some sheets of zinc at my house. We used them to repair the roof of our shed. And soda pop cans are aluminum, aren't they?"

"I think I have a few scraps of copper pipe in the garage," replied Zac.

"The rest sounds like real chemistry stuff," said Marcus. "I know I've used some of it in my science lessons at school."

"Of course! That's it! My old chemistry sets will have that stuff. I'm sure I have some left."

"Great! Anything else?"

"Ah, yes," said Zac. "Arsenic."

"You mean the poison?" Marcus yelped in disbelief.

"Yes, we have a trace of arsenic in our bodies. It's also found in some foods, like Brussels sprouts. They pick it up from the soil in tiny amounts."

"Finally, an excuse not to eat sprouts!" said Marcus.

"There's one thing we can't get, though," said Zac. "Uranium."

"The stuff they make nuclear bombs out of? Yeah, it's probably a good idea that you can't buy that at the store," said Marcus. "I'll just make a little radioactivity sign and stick it on a jar instead. All right, let's get this stuff together!"

The boys gathered all the different elements they could and placed them carefully on the table. Zac measured out small amounts of various powders from his chemistry sets into little glass jars.

"Be careful with these, it's all I have left," he warned.

Just then, there was a knock on the high basement window. Ning waved from outside. Zac opened the window.

"Lucía did it! She can do a cartwheel!" Ning cried.

"Nice work, Lucía!" shouted Zac.

Marcus poked his head around the window frame into the bright sunlight. "Way to go, Lu… Lu…" Just then, he remembered what she had said about bright light making some people sneeze. "AAAACHOOO!"

The explosive sneeze rocked the table, sending the

gathered samples flying in every direction. The table was covered with toppled glassware and spilled powder. Zac and Marcus stared at the disaster in stunned silence.

"Well," said Marcus, "looks like I'll be making a baking soda volcano again, after all."

The friends all laughed.

Meet the Scientists

Wilhelm Roentgen

Wilhelm Roentgen *(REHNT guhn)* (1845–1923) was a German scientist most famous for his discovery of X rays. He also took the first X-ray photographs.

Edward Jenner

Edward Jenner (1749–1823) was an English scientist and doctor who developed the first vaccination. The vaccination inoculated patients against the deadly disease smallpox.

Leonardo da Vinci

Leonardo da Vinci *(lee uh NAHR doh duh VIHN chee)* (1452–1519) was an Italian artist, architect, inventor, scientist, geographer, and engineer. He is perhaps most famous for his painting *Mona Lisa,* but he did important work in a variety of fields.

Anton van Leeuwenhoek

Anton van Leeuwenhoek *(LAY vuhn hook)* (1632–1723) was a Dutch merchant who was one of the first people to observe bacteria. He made drawings of the tiny living things he saw through his microscope.

Rosalind Franklin

Rosalind Franklin (1920–1958) was a British chemist who proved that DNA had a double helix shape. Other scientists relied on her work to continue the study of DNA.

Maurice Wilkins

Maurice Wilkins (1916–2004) was a British scientist who studied the structure of DNA. Wilkins's discoveries helped Crick and Watson build an accurate model of DNA's structure.

Francis Crick

Francis Crick (1916–2004) was a British physicist and biologist. He is best known for his work with James Watson on the structure of DNA.

James Watson

James Watson (1928-   ) is an American biologist best known for the model of the structure of DNA, which he studied and created with the British scientist Francis Crick.

Glossary

bolus   a lump of chewed food mixed with saliva

cochlea   a spiral-shaped, fluid-filled chamber in the inner ear

contract   to draw together, shorten, or shrink

DNA   deoxyribonucleic acid, the main substance through which living things inherit their characteristics

elements, chemical   a substance made up of only one type of atom; one of the basic building blocks of chemistry

greenstick fracture   a break in which the bone is bent and only partly broken

immune   protected from a particular illness or disease

immune system   the parts of the body that protect against disease or illness

inoculate   to protect a person against a disease by placing a weakened form into their bodies

nasal cavity   a large, air-filled space above and behind the nose

nutrients   what your body needs to live; we get nutrients from the food we eat.

olfactory epithelium   a layer of cells at the top of the nasal cavity that detect smells

plasma   the liquid part of blood

retina   the light-sensitive layer at the back of the eyeball

selfie   an informal self-portrait, usually taken with a smartphone

virtual   created and existing only in a computer—like the scenes visited in Zac's Backspace app

X rays   waves of energy that can pass through solid objects

Additional Resources

Books

Body: An Amazing Tour of Human Anatomy
Walker, Richard and Robert Winston (DK Children, 2016)

Human Body A Children's Encyclopedia
(DK Children, 2012)

Stuff You Should Know About the Human Body
Farndon, John (QED Publishing, 2017)

Weird but True! Human Body: 300 Outrageous Facts About Your Awesome Anatomy
(National Geographic Kids, 2017)

Websites

BBC Bitesize – Human Body
https://www.bbc.co.uk/education/topics/zcyycdm

Videos and information about the various parts of the human body.

Kid's Health – How the Body Works
http://kidshealth.org/en/kids/center/htbw-main-page.html?WT.ac=k-nav

Information, videos, and activities about the human body and information on healthy living.

Science for Kids – Human Body Facts
http://www.scienceforkidsclub.com/human-body.html

The different parts of the body explained piece by piece.

Index

9

7